Contents

To Mike, Julia and Ginny

Acknowledgements

The author would like to thank the following people for their help and encouragement in writing this book, and in developing the software.

Stevie Mayhook, RNID for Deaf and Hard of Hearing People

Anne Underwood, BATOD

Joy Jarvis, University of Hertfordshire

Annette Weston, Education Consultant for Sensory Impairment

Karen Rutherford of the B.I.D., Birmingham for her advice on BSL and interpreting work on the CD.

Special thanks to Patrick Sutton for his good-natured patience throughout the software development.

Also special thanks to Linda Evans and her team for their faith in and development of the Word Wheels project.

Word Wheels
interactive CD-ROM

The accompanying CD-ROM contains additional practice exercises for students to use alongside the printed material in the book. They provide opportunities for revision and consolidation, and are ideal for homework as there is British Sign Language (BSL) and audio support for users.

The contents are grouped in three sections:

Section 1: Nouns, articles and plurals
Section 2: Verbs
Section 3: Sentence wheels – allowing the user to compose simple sentences.

All the activities can be marked on screen.
The user (or teacher) can also print out the completed sentences to keep as a record.
Further details can be found on the CD.

Software designed by Patrick Sutton, paddy@lawrence-industrial.co.uk

In order to ensure the successful use of the CD-ROM, the user system requires the following minimum specification:

PC compatible only
Windows 98 SE,NT4 (sp6), XP home and PRO (sp1)
700MHz CPU
128 Mb System memory
32 Mb open GL graphics adapter (Resolution 1027x768)
40 x speed CDROM drive
Sound card installed
Mouse or other pointing device

And optionally:
Printer
Microsoft Word
Active internet connection and browsing software

The project may run on systems below this specification but with some impairment of performance.

Introduction

Originally 'Word Wheels' was conceived as an attempt to respond to the peculiar literacy needs of over-16 profoundly deaf students, whose first language was British Sign Language (BSL); and also those of partially deaf students who used SSE and/or spoken English, and whose knowledge of English grammar was very patchy.

As a Teacher of the Deaf I found that the lack of suitable resources was hindering my work, and therefore the progress of my students.

What was needed was a set of resources for literacy, that would meet the students' specific needs at the right level, and enable them to follow a progressive route to a higher level of literacy skill.

(i) Word Wheels

The title 'Word Wheels' comes from the verb wheel that is included in the pack, both as a template for classroom use and as a feature of the CD.

The verb wheel was originally designed to help deaf students understand the idea of writing a sentence in a particular tense with the correct pronoun agreements.

The third person singular of a verb, in the present simple tense, invariably caused confusion for deaf students due to the 's' ending.

The verb wheel, therefore, offered a visual and tactile method of aligning a suitable time expression, e.g. 'every day', or 'usually', with a choice of personal pronouns, and the correct part of the verb.

In the course of developing this programme, however, it became clear that 'Word Wheels' would be a very useful resource for ESOL/EAL learners, in schools and colleges, as well as for those students who were following the Adult Core Curriculum on Basic Skills/Literacy courses.

(ii) Aims of the Word Wheels Programme

Unit 1

The overall aim of this unit is to teach the student how to build a simple, accurate sentence, by understanding the meaning of basic grammatical terms and how to use them.

Units 2 and 3

The aim of Units 2 and 3 is to help the student to understand more complex sentences and how to write them, by explaining how adjectives, adverbs, object pronouns, and demonstrative adjectives work, in conjunction with further tenses, i.e. the present continuous, the future, the past simple and the past continuous.

BSL students

If you are a BSL user, then you have already mastered one language, and there is no reason why you should not master another.

BSL users will have found, however, that their language does not follow English word order, and therefore writing English may have proved very confusing.

This book adopts a step-by-step approach that sets out each point in a very clear way to avoid confusion. There are plenty of opportunities to practise the lessons on both the worksheets and the CD. The student will find, therefore, that their knowledge increases with every chapter, as does their confidence.

For the deaf BSL user, the aim is:

Firstly – to raise awareness of the structure of written English.

Secondly – to compare it with the different structure of BSL.

The comparative process helps the deaf student to be more aware of errors in his/her written work, and to correct them independently.

ESOL/EAL students

For the student of English as a Foreign Language, the overall aim is to provide the means of acquiring both a basic understanding of English grammatical structure and a familiarity with everyday vocabulary, thus providing the foundation for further study.

The CD contains exercises that are voiced-over, which provides help with pronunciation and intonation.

Basic Skills students

Basic Skills students will find that the Word Wheels Programme can be dipped into as well as studied in depth.

Weak areas can be revised and practised using the book, worksheets and CD, or a combination of the three, depending on the individual needs of students.

The resource book and accompanying worksheets are mapped to the Adult Core Curriculum for Literacy at Entry Levels 1–3, so tutors can select chapters that suit their students' Individual Learning Plans.

How to use the 'Word Wheels' Programme

The Word Wheels Programme contains an illustrated Resource Book with photocopiable worksheets, a template for a verb wheel, and a CD with practice and extension activities.

Resource Book

The book explains systematically, how to put together simple but accurate sentences. Each chapter explains a point of grammar, such as 'nouns', 'verbs', etc., and gives clear examples of the points made, many of which are illustrated for clarity.

The book can be used by tutors and students.

Worksheets and CD

Practice is suggested in either the form of a written worksheet, in which case there will be a worksheet icon 🖹 next to the text; and/or on the CD.

The CD contains extension activities which vary according to difficulty and the amount of help provided. (Please turn to page ix for more information about the CD.)

Activities

There are suggested activities at the end of most chapters to allow the students to explore the material just taught by brainstorming or using their classroom or personal environment.

BSL users

For BSL users there will be some explanations of how sign language differs in structure to most of the grammar taught in this Unit. To indicate those comparisons a thumbs up icon (👍) will be displayed where appropriate.

The CD will provide BSL interpretation of the earlier extension activities as well as a voice-over facility.

Word Wheel

There is a template of the Word Wheel for the present simple tense at the back of the Resource Book. This allows students to manually turn the wheel's circular tiers to produce a correct sentence.

Further practice can be carried out to produce the same results, using the Word Wheels CD included in the pack.

Detailed instructions on how to manipulate the Verb Wheel are given in Chapter 8.

Comparison of English and BSL grammatical structures and terminology

As in any subject you are learning, it is useful to know a few of the special terms, so that you will have a better understanding of what is being referred to.

If you are learning to drive a car, for example, you have to know the names of the different parts of the car, so that you can follow what the instructor is telling you to do.

English, like any language, is made up of different parts, and when all the parts are put together properly, the language, like the car, will run smoothly. The parts of a language and how they fit together are called 'grammar'.

The parts of grammar we are looking at in this Unit are: nouns, pronouns, verbs, articles, and the present simple tense of basic verbs including the verbs 'to be' and 'to have'.

BSL structure

BSL also has parts of grammar, and because both BSL and English are used in England, it is assumed that they will both be exactly the same, and follow the same rules. However, this is not the case.

Example

In English we say or write:

> *John is going to college today* or
> *The car needs new tyres.*

 **In BSL** you sign:

> *John ... college ... go ... today* or
> *car ... new ... tyres ... needs*

Throughout the Word Wheels Programme some of the basic differences between the two languages will be explained and you will be taught how to avoid some of the common errors that are easily made in written English.

Nouns

(i) Introduction

The word 'noun' in English grammar means 'name'.

Nouns are used to name the things we see around us every day, as well as people, places, and animals.

We also give names to our thoughts and feelings.

For example

If I said to you:

> *Please put the 'thing' on the 'thing'*

you would have no idea what I meant. However, if I said to you:

> *Please put the '<u>book</u>' on the '<u>table</u>'*

 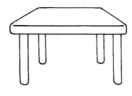

you would know exactly what I meant, and would be able to do it easily.

(ii) Common nouns

The words 'book' and 'table' are both nouns, and they tell you the names of the ordinary things I am talking about, which is why they are called 'common nouns'.

Have a look at some of the things you can see around you almost every day.

For example

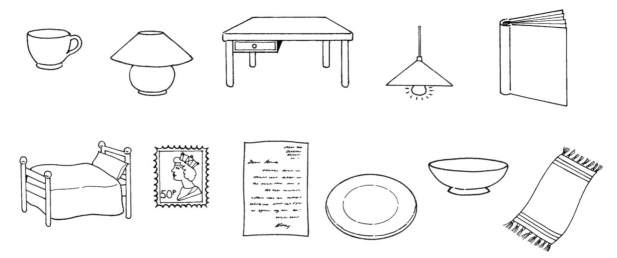

A cup, a lamp, a desk, a light, a book, a bed, a stamp, a letter, a plate, a dish, a rug.

(a) Feelings

We also give names to the thoughts and feelings we have.

For example

Question?	What is the name of the feeling he is having?
Answer	**Happiness or Joy**

Question?	What is the name of the feeling he is having?
Answer	**Unhappiness or Sadness**

Question?	What is this person feeling?
Answer	**Fear or Anxiety**

Question?	What is this person feeling?
Answer	**Anger**

There are many more names for feelings; here are some more examples:

Word		Meaning
Disappointment	–	When something does not happen the way you hoped it would.
Hurt	–	When something or someone upsets you very much by hurting your feelings.
Surprise	–	When something happens that you were not expecting.

(b) Thoughts

We also have names for some kinds of thoughts.

For example

A dream	–	Thoughts that come in pictures when you are asleep.
An idea	–	When you think of something in a new way, or have a plan.
A goal	–	Something you are aiming at and hoping to achieve.
A wish	–	Something you really want to have or to do.

(iii) Proper nouns and the use of capital letters

Ww/E1.2
Rw/E1.3

(a) People

People have names too. You all know the names of your friends and the members of your family.

They all begin with a capital or big letter and are called <u>proper nouns</u>.

Capital letters look like this:

A B C D E F G H I J K L M N O P Q R S T U V W X Y Z

Small letters look like this:

a b c d e f g h i j k l m n o p q r s t u v w x y z

Here are the first names of some of my friends:

<u>A</u>nne, <u>V</u>ickie, <u>P</u>at, <u>R</u>ay, <u>D</u>avid, <u>A</u>shok, <u>J</u>ohn, <u>L</u>ynn

People usually have two or more names.

For example

<u>A</u>nne <u>F</u>iona <u>S</u>mith

<u>R</u>aymond <u>P</u>eter <u>B</u>rannan

Note that a person's name starts with a capital letter, but the rest of the name uses small letters.

'<u>I</u>'

When talking about what '**I**' am doing, I always have to use a **capital '<u>I</u>'**.

Titles

If a person has a title, for example:

Dr (Doctor), Sir, Mrs (Missus), Mr (Mister), Miss, Rev. (Reverend)

then these titles also begin with a capital letter:

<u>D</u>r Peter Collins

<u>M</u>r Larry Hommer

<u>M</u>rs Cathy Lee-Wong

<u>M</u>iss Kay Yuk Ling

<u>R</u>everend James McTavish

(b) Place names

The names of *countries, towns and cities* are all proper nouns,
and use capital letters at the start of their names. For example:

The <u>U</u>nited <u>K</u>ingdom (UK)   <u>I</u>reland

The <u>U</u>nited <u>S</u>tates of <u>A</u>merica (USA)   <u>W</u>ales

<u>F</u>rance   <u>S</u>cotland

<u>I</u>taly   <u>C</u>hina

The United Kingdom is made up of:

<u>S</u>cotland

<u>N</u>orthern <u>I</u>reland

<u>W</u>ales

<u>E</u>ngland

England is made up of many counties or areas:

<u>N</u>orthumberland

<u>Y</u>orkshire

<u>L</u>ancashire

<u>G</u>loucestershire, and many more

In each county there are many towns, cities, and villages.

For example

In **Y**orkshire the names of some of the towns are:

Leeds

Harrogate

York

Otley

Skipton

In each town, city or village, there are streets, roads, avenues and lanes, with different names. As these are also the names of places, they have capital letters at the start of their names as well.

For example

Some street names in **Leeds**:

Buckingham **R**oad

Victoria **R**oad

Headingley **L**ane

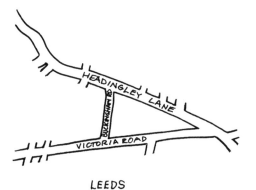

Also in towns and cities there are *special places of interest*. They also are names of places and use capital letters to start their names. For example:

England   [country]

London   [city]

Tower of **L**ondon   [place of interest]

France   [country]

Paris   [city]

Eiffel Tower   [place of interest]

(c) Seas/oceans and rivers

We also give names to the seas, oceans and rivers in the world.

For example

The **P**acific **O**cean

The **A**tlantic **O**cean

The **N**orth **S**ea

The **R**iver **T**hames

The **R**iver **N**ile

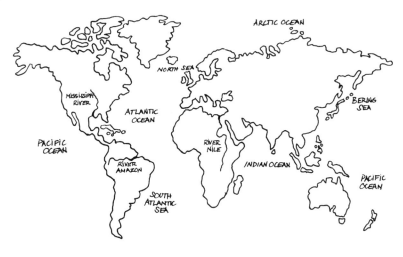

(d) Days of the week

These also have to use a capital letter at the beginning of their names.

<u>M</u>onday

<u>T</u>uesday

<u>W</u>ednesday

<u>T</u>hursday

<u>F</u>riday

<u>S</u>aturday

<u>S</u>unday

(e) Months of the year

The months of the year all need a capital letter at the beginning of their names.

<u>J</u>anuary

<u>F</u>ebruary

<u>M</u>arch

<u>A</u>pril

<u>M</u>ay

<u>J</u>une

<u>J</u>uly

<u>A</u>ugust

<u>S</u>eptember

<u>O</u>ctober

<u>N</u>ovember

<u>D</u>ecember

(f) Special days/times of the year

All special days or special times of the year use a capital letter at the beginning of their names.

<u>C</u>hristmas <u>D</u>ay

<u>P</u>assover

<u>E</u>id

<u>N</u>ew <u>Y</u>ear's <u>D</u>ay

<u>D</u>iwali

<u>E</u>aster <u>D</u>ay

<u>G</u>ood <u>F</u>riday

Note: Always use a capital letter at the beginning of a sentence.

For example

<u>T</u>he holiday is on Friday this year.

<u>M</u>y hotel is very near the beach.

<u>W</u>e see the new puppies every morning.

(iv) Activities

1. Teachers may want to ask students to get into pairs or groups and list as many nouns as possible from their environment.

   This can be a useful vocabulary and spelling activity.

2. Students can exchange information about where they are from, listing their countries', cities' and towns' names. They can then write down their favourite places of interest in this country or their own.

3. Ask students to work in pairs and to name their reaction or feeling if the following events happened to them. Clues can be given.

   1. If you were told you had won ONE MILLION POUNDS.

   2. If you had to stay at work or school for an extra 4 hours.

   3. If you had to cancel your holiday or birthday party.

   4. If some friends from Australia you did not like suddenly arrived at your house to stay for a month.

(v) Worksheets

 Now look at **Worksheets 1 and 2** using the pictures to help you, fill in the gaps in the sentences with the correct nouns.

 Go on to do **Worksheets 3, 4, 5, and 6**. Find as many nouns as you can in the pictures.

 Try **Worksheets 7 and 8** and put in the capital letters where you think they should be.

Articles

(i) Introduction

The words 'A', 'AN' and 'THE' in English are called 'articles'. You may have noticed that when we first looked at nouns, we used 'a' in front of them. In the list of things we could see around us, we wrote:

A chair, **a** table

(ii) Why do we need to write 'A'?

We use 'a' when we mean one of something.

For example

<u>a</u> cup... ...means <u>one</u> cup

<u>a</u> dog... ...means <u>one</u> dog

<u>a</u> cake... ...means <u>one</u> cake

<u>a</u> cup of tea... ...means <u>one</u> cup of tea

We also use 'a' when we do not know which one of something we are talking about.

For example

A bottle of milk... ...means it could be any bottle of milk

A pad of paper... ...means it could be any pad of paper

A Christmas card... ...means it could be any Christmas card

A fish... ...means it could be any fish

Here are some more examples

A man

A house

A temple

A playground

A lesson

an (*x ray*)

(iii) When do we use 'An'?

'An' is used in exactly the same way as 'a', except it is only used in front of words beginning with certain letters.

These letters are **a, e, i, o, u**. They are called **vowels**.

Here are some examples of words beginning with a vowel:

An egg

An orange

An island

An apple

An ice-cube

An eagle

An apron

(iv) Use of the word 'The'

We use '**the**' when we know which particular thing we are talking about.

For example

The bottle of milk is half-empty

We know which bottle of milk we are talking about. It is the one which is half-empty.

Here are some more examples

The boy in the playground is tall

We know which boy, he is the tall one.

The egg is broken

We know which egg we mean, it is the one that is broken.

Have a look at some examples of using 'a' and 'the' together.

1. *'Choose a card'*

It is 'a', because you can choose any card.

2. *'**The** card is **the** ace of spades'*

Here it is '**the**' at the beginning of the sentence, because it is **the** particular card that you have chosen, and also that card is **the** ace of spades.

We know which card it is for two different reasons.

3. *'Can we go on **a** boat?'*

It is 'a' here, because we could go on any of those boats, we do not know which one yet.

4. '**The** boat is very big'

It is 'the' here because we know which boat we are talking about, it is the big one.

5. '**The** girl next door has **a** cat'

It is **'the'** girl, because we know which one, she is the girl next door, but it is **'a'** cat, because we do not know which cat it is.

6. 'Can I buy **a** jacket? **The** flat is very cold'

Here, we do not know which jacket I am going to buy, so it is **'a'**, it could be any one, but we do know which flat, it is the one that is cold, so it is **'the'**.

(v) BSL structure

In BSL you do not sign 'a' 'an' or 'the'.

You would sign, for example:

Bottle – milk – old

The sign for bottle and milk would be made followed by the sign for old, or sour, or horrible, and the facial expression would convey that it was not pleasant to drink.

Card – choose

Again the sign would convey a fan of cards, followed by the sign 'choose' and facial expressions would convey encouragement.

Card – ace – spades

The sign for 'card' would be given or the card pointed to and described as the ace of spades.

Boat – us – can – go?

The eyebrows would be raised to indicate a question, the sign for 'boat' given, followed by the sign for 'us' and 'go'.

Boat – big

The boat would be pointed at and/or the sign for 'boat' would be given, followed by the sign for 'big' which would be emphasised.

(vi) Worksheet

 Now, look at **Worksheet 9**, and choose the right article for each sentence.

Remember to watch out for words starting with vowels, **a, e, i, o, u.**

Plurals

(i) Introduction

The word 'plural' means more than one.

For example, if I say that I have one car, or 'a' car, it is clear how many I have – **one**.

If I say that I have **two cars**, then that is called **the plural**, because it is clear I have more than one car.

In English, the spelling of the noun usually tells you that it is singular or plural.

(ii) How to form the plural of nouns

The normal way to make a single noun into a plural noun, is to add 's'.

Examples

2 chair<u>s</u>

2 dog<u>s</u>

lots of pen<u>s</u>

many book<u>s</u>

Nouns which end with 'ch' or 'sh', add 'es' to make the plural.

For example

1 bush		3 bushes	
1 brush		2 brushes	
1 dish		many dishes	
1 arch		3 arches	
1 witch		3 witches	

1 crutch 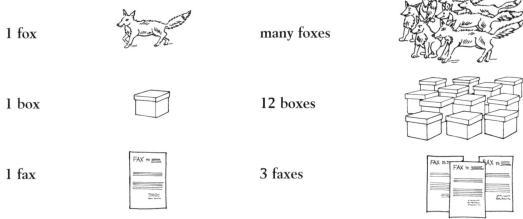 2 crutches

1 watch   2 watches

1 patch   2 patches

Nouns which end in an '**x**' add '**es**' to make the plural.

1 fox   many foxes

1 box   12 boxes

1 fax   3 faxes

Nouns which end in '**f**' or '**fe**', change the '**f**' or '**fe**' to '**ves**' to make the plural.

For example

1 hal<u>f</u> 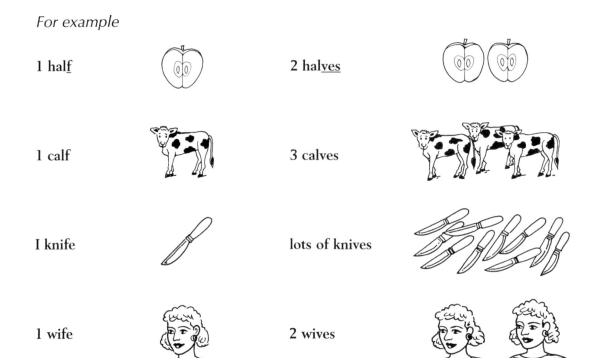 2 hal<u>ves</u>

1 calf   3 calves

I knife   lots of knives

1 wife   2 wives

1 sheaf 6 sheaves

1 leaf 4 leaves

(iii) Other ways of making a plural noun

Some nouns do not follow a rule, and you just have to remember their spellings.

For example

1 man 2 men

1 child 4 children

1 sheep 11 sheep

1 fish 2 fish or fishes

1 tooth 14 teeth

A plural noun does not have to have an exact number in front of it, such as:

4 dogs, **19** doors, **67** cats

It can have words like:

Many	meaning lots
Several	meaning quite a few
Both	meaning two things together
All	meaning everything or everyone
A few	meaning not very many

(iv) 'Some' – the plural of 'A' and 'An'

In Chapter 2 you learnt that 'a' and 'an' meant – **one** thing.

If you wish to make 'a' or 'an' plural, then you write '**some**' in front of the noun.

Remember to make the noun plural as well by changing the spelling.

For example

An egg	some egg<u>s</u>
A watch	some watch<u>es</u>
A child	some child<u>ren</u>

(v) The plural of 'The'

Also in Chapter 2 you learnt to use '**the**' in front of a singular noun, when you knew which noun you were talking about.

'**The**' is also used in front of plural nouns.

For example

The table is big	**The tables are big**
The child is happy	**The children are happy**
The animal is fat	**The animals are fat**

(vi) BSL structure

In BSL the noun stays the same in the plural, and you understand how many there are by the sign that follows.

For example

You would sign:

Chair	2
Dog	many
Pen	9
Table	all

For example, if the phrase was

There are lots of books

the sign order would be

Books – lots

(vii) Activity

Work in pairs or small groups and think of some things in your house, classroom or outside in the street. Make some simple sentences using singular or plural nouns.

Start your list like this:

There *is* – means you are talking about one thing

There *are* – means you are talking about more than one thing

There is a car in the street.

There are two men in the car.

There is a table in the classroom.

There are five classrooms in the school.

(viii) Worksheets

 Have a look at **Worksheet 10** and make the singular nouns into plurals.

 Try **Worksheets 11 and 12**.

Here there is a choice of two spellings for the nouns in each sentence. One is the correct spelling for the singular noun and the other is the correct spelling for the plural.

Read each sentence and decide which spelling is correct and underline it.

Verbs

(i) Introduction

In the first three chapters we have been looking at nouns, why we need them, and at how to make it clear if we mean one thing or more than one thing...i.e. plurals and how to spell them.

Now, however, we need some more 'parts' to be able to build a simple, clear sentence.

The word **'sentence'** has been seen before, but what does it mean?

(ii) What is a sentence?

A sentence is a group of words that make sense.

It starts with a capital or big letter and finishes with a full stop.

For example if I said to you

> *My teacher...*

you would ask, 'Well, what about your teacher?' There is no information there at all. The words do not make any sense.

If I said to you

> *My teacher is young*

now it is clear what I mean.

We have a <u>sentence</u>.

So, what is different?

We have added a **<u>verb</u>** and a word to describe the teacher.

The verb in the sentence is

> *My teacher **<u>is</u>** young*

(iii) BSL structure

In BSL there is no sign for **'is'**.

The word order for the above sentence would be:

> *Teacher – mine – young*   or
>
> *My teacher – young*

(iv) Verbs

<u>Verbs</u> are the next part of grammar we need to understand.

You cannot make a sentence without a verb, so what is it?

(a) What is a verb?

A verb is a word that tells you what someone or something is doing.

Sometimes it is called a '**doing**' word.

Here are some examples:

To walk

To dive

To drive

To jump

To swim

All these words are '**doing**' words.

(v) BSL structure

In BSL the 'action' is usually represented visually by the sign itself.

For example the '**verb**' '**to walk**' is represented by two fingers '**walking**' on the palm of the hand.

The '**verb**' '**to dive**' is represented by two fingers standing on the palm of the hand and then jumping off and falling, the fingers held upright to show the position of 'legs' as they descend.

(b) Unclear verbs

Some verbs are not so clearly 'doing' words, but if you think carefully, someone is doing something.

Here are some examples:

> to dream, to sleep, to wonder, to keep, to have, to wait,
> to see, to fear, to understand, to continue, to wish

When a person is thinking, you cannot see anything happening. Something is happening though. It is the same when a person is dreaming: there is very little action that you can see, but something is happening, isn't it?

Similarly –

You cannot see a person '**seeing**' something.

You cannot see a person '**understanding**' something.

You cannot see a person '**wishing**' for something.

Here are some more examples:

1. The boy **worries**

    The boy is doing something: he is worrying.

2. The ice **melts**

    The ice is doing something: it is melting and becoming water.

3. The child **sleeps**

    The child is doing something: she is sleeping.

4. The old lady **waits**

    The old lady is doing something: she is waiting.

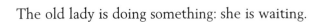

Here are some more examples:

1. He **dies**.
2. Emma **sees** the bus.
3. The people **hope**.
4. The plant **grows**.

5. The man **fears** the dark.

6. The boy **is** naughty.

7. The girl **feels** sad.

8. My sister **has** a new book.

9. David **understands** the lesson.

10. The soldier **wonders** about the future.

Everybody and everything is doing something.

Can you see what is going on in every sentence?

(vi) Activity

1. Have a look around you. What are people doing?

   Make a list of verbs.

   Some people could be:

   Writing

   Reading

   Watching

   Listening

   Signing

   Running

(vii) Worksheet

 Have a look at **Worksheet 13**.

Look at the pictures on this worksheet and list the **'doing' words** or verbs.

Two basic verbs – 'To be' and 'To have' – and pronouns

(i) Introduction

There are two basic verbs in English: they are the verb 'to be' and the verb 'to have'.

These verbs can be used by themselves, but they are also used to help make other tenses for other verbs; so they are often called 'helping' or 'auxiliary' verbs.

(ii) Verb 'To be'

Here is the verb 'to be' written out in full:

I am   *We are*

You are   *They are*

He is

She is

It is

When you say:

I am happy

there is nothing to tell you that anything is happening, but you are doing something, you are **being** happy.

(iii) BSL structure

The verb 'to be' causes a lot of confusion because it does not exist in BSL.

In BSL you do not sign 'am', 'are' or 'is'.

You sign:

Me...happy	Pointing at yourself
He...late	Pointing at the person
Children...beautiful	Sign for children or pointing at children, plus sign 'beautiful'

In English you would write:

> I **am** happy
>
> He **is** late
>
> The children **are** beautiful

Sometimes you will see a name or names instead of a 'he' or 'she', 'it' or 'they'.

This may be confusing at first, but it is simple to work out the correct part of the verb.

For example:

> **Nathan <u>is</u> from Derby**

Nathan is a boy's name, so if we did not use his name, we would say 'he'. Therefore **Nathan** has to take the **'he'** part of the verb which is **'<u>is</u>'**.

Similarly, if we said:

> **Sangeeta <u>is</u> very pretty**

Sangeeta is a girl's name, so if we did not use her name, we would say 'she'. Therefore **Sangeeta** has to take the **'she'** part of the verb, which is **'<u>is</u>'**.

If we wrote:

> **Fiona and Dafyd <u>are</u> very young**

Fiona and Dafyd are two people and so if we did not use their names, we would say **'they'**. Therefore Fiona and Dafyd have to take the **'they'** part of the verb, which is **'<u>are</u>'**.

There is more about pronouns in the next chapter.

(iv) Worksheet

 As the idea of the verb 'to be' may be new, it would be useful to practise for yourself on **Worksheet 14**, so you can become more familiar with how this verb works.

(v) Verb 'To have'

In English the spelling of '**have**' changes with the pronoun/noun.

Here is the verb 'to have' written out in full:

I have	*We have*
You have	*They have*
He has	
She has	
It has	

(vi) BSL structure

The verb '**to have**' is also used in BSL, however the sign '**have**' does not change with the noun or pronoun.

(vii) Worksheet

   Have a look at **Worksheet 14a** to practise using this verb.

Pronouns and verb agreements

(i) Introduction

It is important, when we are looking at how verbs work, to understand something of the little words we use before the verb.

You have already seen **'I'**, **'you'**, **'he'**, **'she'**, **'it'**, **'we'**, and **'they'** in Chapter 5 in connection with the verb 'to be'.

These words are called **'Pronouns'**.

The word 'pronoun' itself, means that it is standing in the place of a noun.

(ii) 'I'

If I am talking about myself, I do not need to repeat my name all the time, I would use 'I'.

For example

I go to school, and I play with my friends.

I swim on Tuesday and I go to bed early.

(iii) 'You' – singular and plural

If I am talking to one other person or a group of people, I wouldn't need to use their name or names, I would use **'you'** both times.

For example

You can catch the early bus.

You are late.

Sometimes you can add the name of the person you are talking to for emphasis. It can go at the end or the beginning of the sentence.

For example

> <u>You</u> can catch the early bus, Mike.
>
> Mike, <u>you</u> can catch the early bus.
>
> <u>You</u> are late, Mike.
>
> Mike, <u>you</u> are late.

The word 'you' can mean **one** person, or **more than one** person.

Here are some examples of 'you' in the singular and plural:

You are my friend

You are my friends

You have to be back by 5 o'clock

You have to be back by 6 o'clock

(iv) He/She

If I am talking about my friend, and what he/she is doing, you really do not want to read:

> Hajid goes to town. Hajid buys a cake.   or
>
> Gwyneth goes to college. Gwyneth has a music lesson.

It looks very boring doesn't it?

So, after I have said my friend's name once, and have said

> Hajid goes to town...
>
> Gwyneth goes to college...

I can continue with:

> ...he buys a cake
>
> ...she has a music lesson

The full sentences then look like this

> Hajid goes to town, he buys a cake.
>
> Gwyneth goes to college, she has a music lesson.

(v) 'It'

If I am talking about something that is not a person, for example 'a shop', I would use 'it', instead of repeating the words 'the shop'.

For example

1. The shop is always open at night, <u>it</u> sells fresh vegetables.

   The '<u>it</u>' refers to the shop.

2. The classroom is big, <u>it</u> has many desks.

   The '<u>it</u>' refers to the classroom.

We also use '<u>it</u>' for animals.

For example

> The horse runs in the field, <u>it</u> is very fast.
>
> The elephant is very big, <u>it</u> is also very slow.
>
> I see the cat, <u>it</u> is asleep.
>
> The tiger walks slowly, <u>it</u> jumps on to the rock.

(vi) 'We'

If I am talking about my friend and myself, I would use 'we' instead of using our names all the time.

For example

I would start the sentence using the name of my friend and 'I':

> Ian and I went to see a film, <u>we</u> enjoyed it.
>
> Anne and I met the teacher, <u>we</u> said, 'Hello'.
>
> Zawhora and I read the book, <u>we</u> liked it.

(vii) 'They'

If I am talking about other people, for example, Anne and Zawhora, I would use '<u>they</u>'.

For example

> Anne and Zawhora read the book, <u>they</u> liked it.
>
> Julia and Hajid went to town, <u>they</u> had a coffee.

(viii) Worksheets

 Now have a look at **Worksheets 15 and 16**.

 In **Worksheet 15** look at the sentences carefully and fill in the gaps with the correct form of the verb that goes with each noun or pronoun.

 In **Worksheet 16** fill in the gaps with a pronoun/noun or a name/s.

7 Verb tenses

(i) Introduction

As you have seen now, verbs are 'doing' words, telling the reader what is happening.

So far we have used them with a noun, so the reader knows who or what is doing the action.

Have a quick look at this sentence just to revise:

The lady drives the car

We know **what the action is**, it's:

      drives   [verb]

We know who is doing the action, it's:

      the lady   [noun]

In English, we can show by the spelling of the verb **when the action takes place**.

Showing **when** the action takes place is called a '<u>tense</u>'.

Tense

The word '**tense**' simply means 'time'.

There are three main tenses in English, they are:

(ii) The present tense

This is used when we are talking about actions that are going on now, or regularly. It is also called the '<u>present simple tense</u>'.

(iii) The future tense

This is used for actions that have not happened yet, they may happen at another time in the future – for example, tomorrow, or next week.

(iv) The past tense

This tense is used for actions which happened in the past. These actions are finished, they are no longer happening. They could have happened last week, or yesterday, or any time in the past.

(v) The present simple tense

In the last few chapters we have only used the **present simple tense**, and you have seen examples written like this:

The cat <u>sleeps</u>

The tiger <u>jumps</u>

You <u>read</u>

Here is a verb written out in full in the present simple tense:

The verb 'to walk'

I walk	We walk
You walk	They walk
He walk<u>s</u>	
She walk<u>s</u>	
It walk<u>s</u>	

You can see that for the part of the verb that goes with:

he

she

it

the verb spelling changes and an '<u>s</u>' is added.

Here is another example:

The verb 'to run'

I run	We run
You run	They run
He run<u>s</u>	
She run<u>s</u>	
It run<u>s</u>	

(vi) Activity 1

Here are some pictures of people doing things.

Can you write a simple sentence saying what the people are doing in each picture?

Here is an example:

The verb is 'to cook'   The man cooks

1. The verb is 'to wash'   _____

2. The verb is 'to skate'   _____

3. The verb is 'to swim'   _____

When the verb is written in the present simple tense as in the examples in this chapter, it shows that the action is something that happens regularly, in the present time.

This tense can also be used to tell a story or 'narrative'.

(vii) The present simple tense and time phrases

When something is happening, the reader has to know when it happens, or how often it happens, and 'time phrases' give that information.

Here are some examples:

Every day
Usually
Generally
} these mean most of the time

Often
Sometimes
} these mean some of the time

All of these phrases tell the reader that something happens quite regularly.

Here are some sentences in the present simple tense using some time phrases.

> I *often swim* in the sea.
> Habib *goes* to school *every day*.
> She *telephones* her mother in the *evenings*.
> Mr Patel *works* in the city *sometimes*.
> The shops *open every Saturday*.
> The doctor *sees* his patients *every morning*.

Can you see that the verbs plus the underlined time phrases, all tell you that something is happening regularly?

The present simple tense can also be used, as we said before, to tell a story.

(viii) Activity 2

1. Read the story below.

2. Underline all the verbs you can see in the present simple tense, and any time phrases as well.

3. Make a list of the verbs you have underlined.

Story

The man <u>thinks</u> there <u>is</u> nobody in the house. He goes to the back door. He opens it carefully. He looks inside the kitchen. The man knows that the lady sometimes goes to church on Sundays.

When he is sure that the lady is out, he steals her purse, and runs away. He runs into the street and bumps into a little boy. The boy cries and his mother comes to help him. She shouts at the man.

(ix) Worksheets

 Have a look at **Worksheets 17 and 18**.

Fill in the correct part of the verb to match the person doing the action.

The verbs are:

To read	To swim
To run	To climb
To iron	To eat
To sleep	To kick

You will see that they are all either 'he' or 'she'.

8 The Wheel Wheel

The Word Wheel

In Appendix 1, there is a pattern for a **'word wheel'**.

The wheel is designed to help you make some simple sentences in the present simple tense.

(ii) How to use the wheel

1. Look at the smallest circle first – choose a time phrase.

2. Look at the next circle – choose who is doing the action, 'I', 'you', 'he', etc.

3. Choose a verb from the outer circle.

4. Match the right part of the verb with the right person, 'I build' but '<u>he</u> build<u>s</u>'.

5. Complete the sentence by choosing a suitable noun.

(iii) Worksheets

 On **Worksheet 19a** you will see some nouns, time phrases, and verbs.

 Using **Worksheet 19b** and the **Word Wheel**, try to match up the pronouns, verbs, nouns and time phrases from **Worksheet 19a** to make up some simple sentences.

For example

You will see some **nouns**:

> *A lorry, a friend, a song*

Some **time phrases**:

> *Every week, often, sometimes*

Some **verbs**:

> *To see, to drive, to sing*

Your sentences could be:

1. Sometimes I see a friend.

2. Often I sing a song.

3. Every week I drive a lorry.

Finally have a look at Worksheet 20.

See if you can explain what the grammar terms mean.

See the Answer Sheet on page 64.

(iv) Conclusion

You have now completed Unit 1 of the Word Wheels Programme and have learnt how to build a simple sentence in English, using basic grammar and simple words.

The CD has further exercises to help you to practise the lessons you have learnt, before you go on to build more complicated sentences in Unit 2.

The exercises on the CD are graded according to difficulty, with the earlier activities providing considerable support (BSL, audio, pictures, words).

Appendix 1: Word Wheel templates

Photocopy the three discs on the next two pages and cut them out. Using different coloured card can be useful, and laminating the discs will extend the life of the 'wheel'. Fasten together with a butterfly pin to make the Word Wheel, allowing pupils to turn individual circles and compose a variety of sentences.

The completed Word Wheel will look like this.

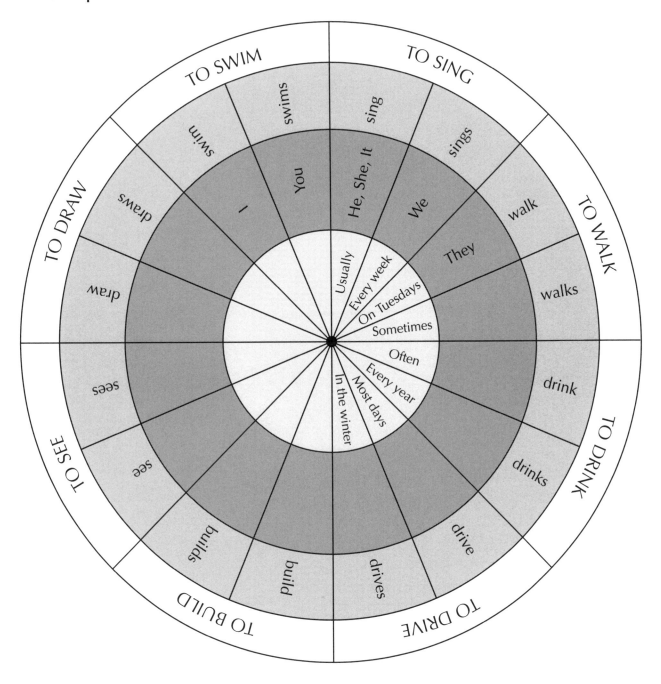

Middle circle

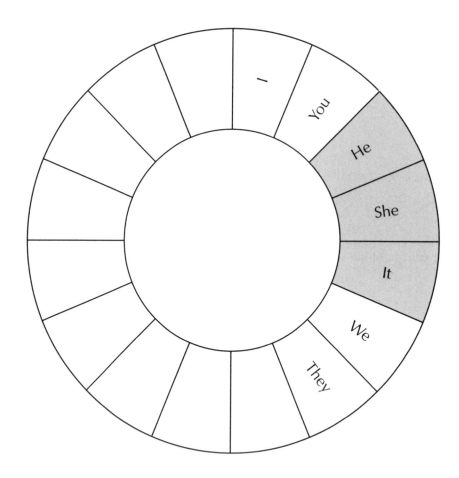

Inner circle

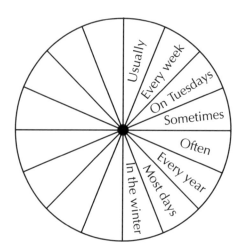

Outer circle

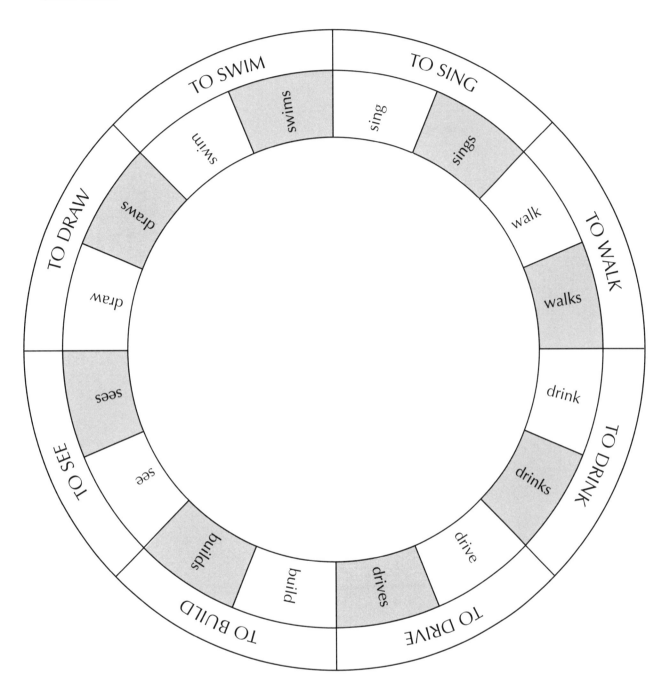

Appendix 2:
Worksheets 1 to 20

Worksheet 1

Look at the pictures and put the correct nouns in the gaps in the sentences.

1. The .... runs fast.

2. The .... cries.

3. The .... is very old.

4. My .... is new.

5. Our .... is asleep.

Worksheet 2

Here are some more sentences.

Look at the pictures and put the correct nouns in the gaps.

1. I have a new ....

2. Where is your blue ....?

3. The .... has got a hole in it.

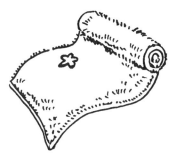

4. The .... is very fresh.

5. The .... is in the room.

Worksheet 3

Here we are looking at the nouns that you can see in different places.

Have a look at the pictures and try to write down as many nouns as you can.

You may like to work in pairs and use a dictionary to check your spellings.

Here are two examples.

$$2 \times 2 = 4$$
$$3 \times 3 = 9$$
$$4 \times 4 = 16$$

1. a board

2. a computer

3. ....

4. ....

5. ....

6. ....

7. ....

8. ....

9. ....

10. ....

Worksheet 4

Look at the picture.

How many nouns can you find?

Make a list.

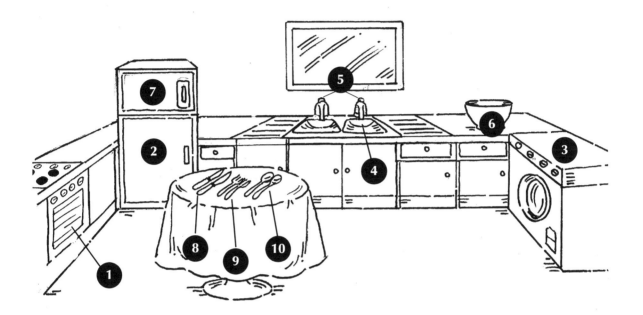

1.   ....

2.   ....

3.   ....

4.   ....

5.   ....

6.   ....

7.   ....

8.   ....

9.   ....

10.   ....

Worksheeet 5

Look at the picture.

How many nouns can you find?

Make a list.

1. ....

2. ....

3. ....

4. ....

5. ....

6. ....

7. ....

8. ....

9. ....

10. ....

Worksheet 6

Have a look at the picture.

How many nouns can you find?

Make a list.

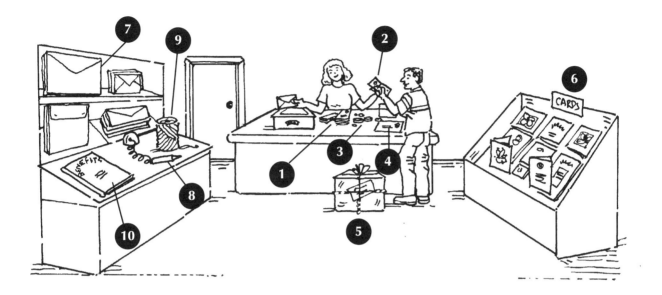

1. ....

2. ....

3. ....

4. ....

5. ....

6. ....

7. ....

8. ....

9. ....

10. ....

Worksheet 7

Look at the sentences below.

Circle the words that should have a capital letter.

1.   john and helen want to go to london.

2.   can i see the film on thursday?

3.   i like to visit my friend sharon in birmingham.

4.   it always rains when i go to france in august.

5.   the new houses in winford road were very big.

6.   we saw lots of elephants in africa last may.

7.   the party on christmas day is usually very nice.

8.   my sister rachel is coming to stay.

9.   mrs patel lives with her mother at 34 westhill road.

10. the children love to swim in the atlantic ocean.

Worksheet 8

Look at the sentences below.

Circle the letters that should be capital letters.

1. on monday rashid went to see the doctor.

2. dr singh is always on time.

3. when can we see mrs harrison's new baby?

4. sanjay wants to visit the tower of london in july.

5. which day is easter day this year?

6. all my students want to visit america this summer.

7. alan's new dog is called 'henry'.

8. the smith family generally goes to spain every year.

9. have you got tickets for 'hamlet' this june?

10. please tell joe that i only drink tea.

Worksheet 9

Look at the following sentences.

The articles are missing.

Put 'a', 'an' or 'the' in the gaps in the sentences.

Remember to use the right article before a word beginning with a vowel, a, e, i, o, u.

Example

1. **Would you like . . . an . . . egg?**

2. Has he got .... money I sent?

3. .... film we saw yesterday was very good.

4. Can I have .... coffee?

5. Buy .... new jumper, it is cold.

6. Have you got .... pound, please?

7. Have .... cake, they are nice.

8. I need .... book I gave you.

9. Would you like .... orange?

10. There is .... bird on the grass.

Worksheet 10

Look at the following list of nouns.

Make them into plurals.

Example

1.	1 <u>table</u>	2 table<u>s</u>
2.	a cat	lots of ....
3.	a pen	many ....
4.	one teacher	8 ....
5.	a girl	4 ....
6.	a computer	some ....
7.	a chair	5 ....
8.	a lamp	2 ....
9.	1 brother	4 ....
10.	a bath	2 ....

Worksheet 11

Look at the sentences below.

Read each sentence and decide if the singular or plural noun is correct.

Underline the right word.

Example

1. **I have one <u>pen</u>/pens in my bag.**

   The right word is 'pen' as it says 'I have one'.

2. She has two cat/cats at home.

3. We have some box/boxes at home.

4. I see four fox/foxes in the garden.

5. The three bush/bushes are small.

6. I need a new brush/brushes.

7. The church has an old arch/arches.

8. We need a lot of chair/chairs in the room today.

9. The teacher has only one desk/desks.

10. The car has a new wheel/wheels.

Worksheet 12

Look at the sentences.

Underline the correct word in each sentence as in Worksheet 11.

1. Mrs Jones now has five child/children.

2. The boys want more toy/toys.

3. I can see one lady/ladies in the shop.

4. You can have three wish/wishes on your birthday.

5. Can I have a new patch/patches on my trousers?

6. Please send the two fax/faxes on my desk.

7. Do you want an extra knife/knives for your food?

8. How many man/men are on the bus?

9. There are six bird/birds on the grass.

10. Have some sandwich/sandwiches.

Worksheet 13

Look at the pictures below.

List as many 'doing' words/verbs as you can.

Example

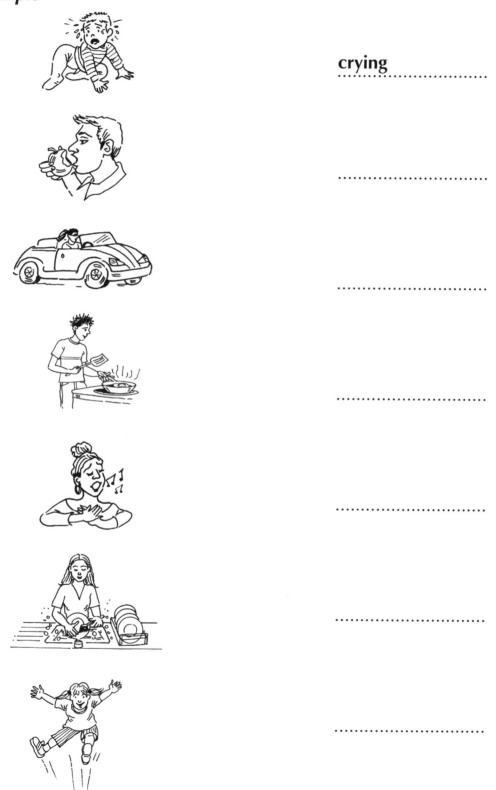

crying

....

....

....

....

....

....

....

Worksheeet 14

Look at the sentences below.

Fill in the gaps with the correct part of the verb 'to be'.

Choose from:

'am' 'are' 'is'

1. We .... always late for the bus.

2. I .... pleased to meet you.

3. He .... a very good student.

4. You .... all welcome at the college.

5. Christina and Javid .... very hard-working.

6. You and I .... very lucky today.

7. Salna .... from Pakistan.

8. She .... not very happy at the moment.

9. The lady in the café .... old.

10. The cat .... frightened of loud noises.

Worksheet 14a

Look at the following sentences.

Fill in the gaps with the correct part of the verb 'to have'.

Example

I .... a new car.   I **have** a new car.

1. You .... a lovely garden.

2. Dylan .... some new shoes.

3. My mother .... the car today.

4. Javid's sister .... many friends here.

5. The desk .... a broken drawer.

6. Amir and I .... a meeting at 6 o'clock.

7. All my friends .... new jobs.

8. Sanjay .... a new baby brother.

9. The house .... two garages.

10. Mrs Jones .... three grandchildren.

Worksheet 15

Now try to fill in the gaps in the following sentences with the correct part of the verb.

There are no clues to help this time.

1. I .... with the ball.   (to play)

2. She .... in town in the evening.   (to stay)

3. Salna .... a new bicycle for his birthday.   (to want)

4. Mrs Jones .... her friend to dinner.   (to ask)

5. Joe .... a long way to work.   (to travel)

6. The girls .... very hard in the summer.   (to work)

7. The dog .... the cat in the garden.   (to watch)

8. The birds .... in the early morning.   (to sing)

9. Hussein and I .... to swim on holiday.   (to like)

10. You .... to come to school earlier.   (to need)

Worksheet 16

Look at the sentences below.

Fill in the gaps with a pronoun/noun or name/names to match the verb.

Example

.... play<u>s</u> with the children.

There is an 's' ending to the verb, so you could write, '<u>he</u>', '<u>she</u>' or '<u>it</u>'. You could also make up a name and say:

'<u>*Amir*</u>' plays with the children.

1. .... eats a big meal every day.

2. .... always go to the swimming baths on Sunday.

3. .... never arrive early for my lessons.

4. .... sing with my friend in the choir.

5. .... is the best singer in the school.

6. .... are happy in the zoo.

7. .... swims very well.

8. .... am very busy at the moment.

9. .... stays in town at the weekend.

10. .... want new toys for their birthdays.

Worksheet 17

Look at the pictures and decide what verb is being used. (There is a list on page 33.)

Write down the correct part of the verb next to the picture.

Example

1. **He <u>reads</u>**

2. She ....

3. She ....

4. He ....

Worksheet 18

Look at the pictures and decide what the verb is. (There is a list on page 33.)

Write the correct part of the verb next to the picture.

1. He ....

2. He ....

3. She ....

4. He ....

Worksheet 19a

Nouns

a house, a wall, a picture, a mile, a lorry,

a kilometre, a beer, a friend, a car,

a horse, the baby, a lemonade, a song, some snow, a girl.

Time Phrases

In the winter, Usually, On Tuesdays, Often,

Every week, Sometimes, Every year, Most days.

Verbs

to sing, to drink, to walk, to draw, to swim,

to drive, to build, to see

Now you are going to try to make up sentences using the words that you have been given in the groups above.

Worksheet 19b

Example

1. Choose a time phrase.

2. Use your Word Wheel and choose a verb.

3. Make the verb match the person doing the action.

4. Choose a noun. You can write it in the singular or make it plural.

Examples

1. Sometimes <u>we</u> <u>sing</u> songs.

2. Every week <u>he</u> <u>drinks</u> a beer.

3. On Tuesdays <u>we</u> <u>swim</u> a mile.

4. In the winter <u>they</u> <u>drive</u> 30 kilometres.

Now, have a go yourself.

1. ....

2 ....

3. ....

4. ....

5. ....

6. ....

Worksheet 20

Grammar Assessment

You have now reached the end of Unit 1. Well done!

Before you begin the next Unit of Word Wheels, check that you have understood the new grammar terms that you have learnt.

Explain briefly what the following words mean:

A Noun ....

A Verb ....

A Pronoun ....

An Article ....

A Tense ....

The Present Simple Tense ....

....

Singular ....

Plural ....

Answers

Noun	The name of a 'thing', a place, a person.
Verb	A 'doing' or 'action' word.
Pronoun	**'I', 'he', 'she,' 'it', 'you', 'we', 'they'**. These are words which stand in the place of nouns.
Articles	**'a', 'an', 'the'**.
Tense	This tells the reader when the action happened.
Present Simple	This tense is used when the action happens regularly, or in a story.
Singular	This means one of something.
Plural	This means more than one thing.